End of Life Plan

Written by

_____

Note:
This is NOT a legal document and does not replace any wills or other documentation mentioned herein.

Copies of this journal are here:

_____

_____

_____

_____

_____

_____

To those who read this journal

Personal Information

Personal Information

Full legal name

Maiden surname

Known to most as

Nicknames

Birth date

Place of birth

Personal Identification Numbers	
ID Number	
Where to find it	
Tax Number	
Where to find it	
Passport Number	
Where to find it	

Personal Information

Qualifications

My Religion and involvement

Other

Personal Information

(Additional space has been provided so that you can keep this information up to date)

Postal Address	PO Box key is located

Dates at this address: From _____ to _____

Postal Address	PO Box key is located

Dates at this address: From _____ to _____

Postal Address	PO Box key is located

Dates at this address: From _____ to _____

Postal Address	PO Box key is located

Dates at this address: From _____ to _____

Personal Information

(Additional space has been provided so that you can keep this information up to date)

Physical Address

Dates at this address: From _____ to _____

Physical Address

Dates at this address: From _____ to _____

Physical Address

Dates at this address: From _____ to _____

Physical Address

Dates at this address: From _____ to _____

Personal Information

Telephone Number	
Mobile Number	Provider
Other contact numbers	

Email address	Access via	Password

Notes

My Family

A copy of my **family tree** is located

My Parents		
Mother	Born	Died
Father	Born	Died
Where married	Date	Divorced
More about my parents		

My Spouse/s			
Name		Born	Died
Where we were married		Date	Divorced
Name		Born	Died
Where we were married		Date	Divorced
Name		Born	Died
Where we were married		Date	Divorced

My Children

Name		Born
School		
Allergies & Medications	Doctor	Dr Tel
Other		

Name		Born
School		
Allergies & Medications	Doctor	Dr Tel
Other		

Name		Born
School		
Allergies & Medications	Doctor	Dr Tel
Other		

Name		Born
School		
Allergies & Medications	Doctor	Dr Tel
Other		

My Grandchildren

Name	Born
Parents	
Name	Born
Parents	
Name	Born
Parents	
Name	Born
Parents	
Name	Born
Parents	
Name	Born
Parents	
Name	Born
Parents	
Name	Born
Parents	
Name	Born
Parents	

My Pets

Vet	Vet Tel

Pet care arrangements on my passing

_____

_____

_____

_____

_____

_____

_____

_____

_____

_____

_____

_____

_____

_____

My Pets

Name	Breed

Special Instructions

Name	Breed

Special Instructions

Name	Breed

Special Instructions

Name	Breed

Special Instructions

My Pets

Name	Breed

Special Instructions

Name	Breed

Special Instructions

Name	Breed

Special Instructions

Name	Breed

Special Instructions

Notes

Notes

Medical
Information

Medical Information

Medical Aid	Policy Number
Contact No	

Notes

In the event that I become incapacitated

My Blood Type	
Hospital of Choice	Contact
My nominated health care power of attorney is	Contact

The health care power of attorney document is located

My living will can be found

My Do Not Resuscitate document can be found

My Organ Donor document can be found

My Doctors

GP Name	Contact Number
Notes	

Specialist Name	Contact Number
Type of specialist	
Notes	

Specialist Name	Contact Number
Type of specialist	
Notes	

Specialist Name	Contact Number
Type of specialist	
Notes	

My Medical History

Condition	When diagnosed	Treatment

Family Medical History

On my Mother's side	On my Father's side
My mother died of	My father died of

My Children's Medical History

Child's Name	Condition	When diagnosed	Treatment

Notes

Notes

Funeral
Arrangements

Planning My Funeral

I have a funeral policy with

Policy Number	Amount	Contact

Other Policies to cover my funeral

Policy with	Amount	Contact	Notes

My preferred **funeral home** is	

I would like to be

☐ **Buried** at this cemetery	☐ **Cremated** and my ashes disposed of here

Notes for gravestone	

Planning My Funeral

Special Notes for the Day
(e.g. who I would like to lead the service, music or hymns I like, special requests)

Planning My Funeral

Special Notes for the Day
(e.g. who I would like to lead the service, music or hymns I like, special requests)

Contact
Information

Important Contacts

Who	Name	Number / Email	Note
Pastor / Spiritual Leader			
Attorney			
Bank			
Doctor			
Employer			
Funeral Home			
Funeral Policy			
Executor			

Family Members

Name	Number / Email	Note

Family Members

Name	Number / Email	Note

Friends

Name	Number / Email	Note

Friends

Name	Number / Email	Note

Associates, Colleagues & Acquaintances

Who	Name	Number / Email	Note

Associates, Colleagues & Acquaintances

Who	Name	Number / Email	Note

Documents

Important Documents

What	Where to find it	Note
Last Will & Testament		
ID Document		
Passport		
Birth Certificate		
Marriage Certificate		
Medical Insurance		
Tax Documents		
Driver's License		
Children's Birth Certificates		
Life Policy 1:		
Life Policy 2:		
Life Policy 3:		
Funeral Policy 1:		
Funeral Policy 2:		
Short Term Policy 1:		
Short Term Policy 2:		

Important Documents

What	Where to find it	Note
Home Owner's Policy:		
Deeds to Property 1:		
Deeds to Property 2:		
Deeds to Property 3:		
Bank Card 1:		
Bank Card 2:		
Bank Card 3:		
Website / Social Media Access & Passwords		
Pet Records		
Photo Albums – Printed		
Photo Albums - Digital		
Farewell letters to loved ones		

Important Documents

Website/Internet Site	Password	Note

Notes

Finances

My Estate Custodians

The Executor of my estate is	
Contact	The signed order can be found

I have nominated this person to hold Power of Attorney	
Contact	The signed order can be found

Special Notes to my Estate Custodians

Bank Accounts

Type	Institution	Account Number	Contact	Notes
Credit Card				
Checking Acc				
Savings Acc				
Debit Card				
Pension Fund				

Fixed Assets

What	Where to find the paperwork	Contact	Notes

Investments

What	Where to find the paperwork	Contact	Notes

Income

Who	What for	Amount	Contact	Notes
	Pension			
	Grants			
	Property Rental			
	Salary			

Money I am Owed

Who	What for	Amount	Contact	Notes

Debt & Liabilities

What	Where to find the paperwork	Contact	Notes
Mortgage			
Vehicle Loan			
Credit Card			
Retail Account 1:			
Retail Account 2:			

Bills

Who	What for	Approx. Amount	Contact	Notes
	Mortgage			
	Vehicle			
	School Fees			
	Loan			
	Utilities			
	Internet			
	Mobile Contract			

Notes

Notes

Loose Ends

Where to find my...

What	Where	Notes
Address Book		
House Keys		
Car Keys		
Safe Key		
Safety Deposit Key		
Important Documents	*(see Documents)*	
Safe		
Jewelry		
Heirlooms		
Collectables		

Services to Close and Cancel

Service	Account #	Contact	Website	Access Info
P O Box				
Mobile				
Utilities				
Magazine				
Newspaper				
Cleaners				
Groomers				
Garden Service				
Gym Membership				
Television				

Services to Close and Cancel

Service	Account #	Contact	Website	Access Info

Special Requests for my belongings

Notes

These people know about this journal

A note to the beneficiaries listed in my Will

Last Thoughts

Made in the USA
Las Vegas, NV
03 January 2024

83865162R00042